1970

YOU M~~UST REMEMBER~~ THIS

MILESTONES, MEMORIES,
TRIVIA AND FACTS, NEWS EVENTS,
PROMINENT PERSONALITIES &
SPORTS HIGHLIGHTS OF THE YEAR

TO : _____

FROM : _____

MESSAGE : _____

_____

*selected and researched
by
mary a. pradt*

WARNER ⓦ TREASURES™

PUBLISHED BY WARNER BOOKS

A TIME WARNER COMPANY

COPYRIGHT ©1995
by Mary A. Pradt
All Rights Reserved.

Warner Books, Inc.
1271 Avenue of the Americas
New York, New York 10020

Warner Treasures is a
trademark of Warner Books, Inc.

A Time Warner Company

DESIGN:
CAROL BOKUNIEWICZ DESIGN
PRINTED IN SINGAPORE
FIRST PRINTING : MAY 1995
10 9 8 7 6 5 4 3 2 1
ISBN : 0-446-91047-3

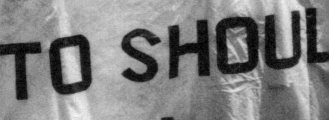

President Richard Nixon ordered the bombing of Cambodia. Several student protests took place around the country as a reaction to his decision. During a May 4 demonstration at **Kent State** University in Ohio national guardsmen killed 4 students. Ten days later, 2 more students were killed at Jackson State College in Mississippi.

The Atomic Energy Commission reported that during the year it had held 24 underground nuclear tests at a site in Nevada.

On April Fools' Day, President Nixon signed a bill banning cigarette advertising on television and radio.

EXPO 70 — THE WORLD'S FAIR — OPENED IN OSAKA, JAPAN.

More than one million cans of **tuna fish** were recalled by the government in December because of mercury contamination, causing the canning industry an estimated $44 million in losses.

Velazquez's portrait of Juan de Pareja sold at Christie's in London for $5,540,000.

The world's most valuable stamp, the 1856 British Guiana one-cent, sold at auction for $280,000.

The price of **gold** on the free market fell below the official price of $35 an ounce.

Oleomargarine heir **Michael Brody** was besieged with requests after he announced he would give away part of his $6.8 million inheritance.

cultural milestones

The US census showed the smallest number of men (94.8) in ratio to women (100) in history.

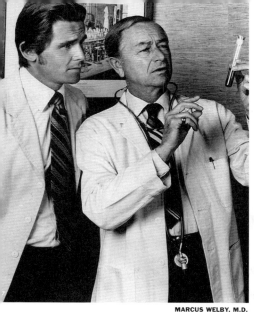

MARCUS WELBY, M.D.

television

Almost 40 percent of TV households now had color TV.

Only 7.6% of TV households subscribed to cable systems. There were almost 60 million TV households in America. Worldwide, there were an estimated 231 million sets.

TOP-RATED TV SHOWS OF 1970

1. "Marcus Welby, M.D." (ABC)
2. "The Flip Wilson Show" (NBC)
3. "Here's Lucy" (CBS)
4. "Ironside" (NBC)
5. "Gunsmoke" (CBS)
6. "ABC Movie of the Week" (ABC)
7. "Hawaii Five-O" (CBS)
8. "Medical Center" (CBS)
9. "Bonanza" (NBC)
10. "The FBI" (ABC)
11. "Mod Squad" (ABC)
12. "Adam-12" (NBC)
13. "Rowan & Martin's Laugh-In" (NBC) tied with
14. "Wonderful World of Disney" (NBC)
15. "Mayberry R.F.D." (CBS)
16. "Hee Haw" (CBS)

Woody Woodpecker got his own Saturday morning TV show. And on September 12, 1970, "Josie and the Pussycats," a Hanna-Barbera cartoon, debuted on CBS.

MOD SQUAD

JANIS JOPLIN

milestones

DEATHS

Janis Joplin, rock and roll singer, 27, died of a heroin overdose in Hollywood October 4.

Jimi Hendrix, legendary rock and roll guitarist, 27, overdosed on drugs in London on September 18.

Billie Burke, actress famous for her role as Glenda the Good Witch in *The Wizard of Oz* (1939), died at 84.

Louise Bogan, American poet, died at 72.

Marie Dionne, frailest of the Dionne quints, died at 35.

Erle Stanley Gardner, the author, died at 80.

Rube Goldberg, cartoonist, died at 87.

Johnny Hodges, alto saxophone great of the Duke Ellington Orchestra, died at 63.

Gypsy Rose Lee, famed stripper, died at 56.

Oscar Lewis, author and anthropologist, died at 55.

Sonny Liston, boxer, died at 38.

Yukio Mishima, Japanese author, committed ritual suicide, hara-kiri, at age 45.

Mark Rothko, American abstract painter, died at 66.

Bertrand Russell, philosopher and mathematician, died at 97.

Abraham Zapruder, who took the famous film of the Kennedy assassination, died August 30 at the age of 66.

John O'Hara, novelist and art critic, died September 28.

celeb births

RIVER PHOENIX, the late actor, was born August 23.
MALCOLM JAMAL WARNER, actor, was born August 18.
ANDRE AGASSI, tennis star, was born April 29.
KIRK CAMERON, actor, was born October 12.
DEBBIE GIBSON, singer and songwriter, was born August 31.

celeb weddings

SINGER SAMMY DAVIS, JR., 44, married third wife **ALTAVISE GORE,** the captain of his dancing troupe, in Philadelphia on May 11.

Comedian **JACKIE GLEASON,** 54, married **BEVERLY MCKITTRICK** in a civil ceremony in Ashford, England, on July 4, just days after his divorce from Genevieve Halford Gleason.

Gamine actress **MIA FARROW,** 25, married **ANDRE PREVIN,** 40, the principal conductor of the London Symphony Orchestra, on September 10 in London. Mia was divorced from first husband Frank Sinatra.

70's hit music

1. **bridge over troubled water** Simon and Garfunkel
2. **i'll be there** Jackson Five
3. **raindrops keep fallin' on my head** B. J. Thomas
4. **close to you** Carpenters
5. **my sweet lord/isn't it a pity** George Harrison
6. **i think i love you** Partridge Family
7. **ain't no mountain high enough** Diana Ross
8. **american woman/no sugar tonight** Guess Who
9. **war** Edwin Starr
10. **let it be** Beatles

Other chart-topping musical memories: **"Make It With You"** by Bread **"Fire and Rain"** by James Taylor **"In the Summertime"** by Mungo Jerry and **"Whole Lotta Love"** by Led Zeppelin. Simon and Garfunkel also released **"Cecilia."** Chicago issued **"25 or 6 to 4."** John Ono Lennon, former Beatle, recorded the wonderful **"Instant Karma (We All Shine On),"** which peaked at #3.

The Beatles also had a #1 hit with "The Long and Winding Road / For You Blue." **The Jackson Five** had other #1 singles — "ABC," "The Love You Save / I Found that Girl," and "I Want You Back."

bestselling

fiction

1. **love story**
   by erich segal
2. **the french lieutenant's woman**
   by john fowles
3. **islands in the stream**
   (posthumous) by ernest hemingway
4. **the crystal cave**
   by mary stewart
5. **great lion of god**
   by taylor caldwell
6. **qb vii**
   by leon uris
7. **the gang that couldn't shoot straight**
   by jimmy breslin
8. **the secret woman**
   by victoria holt
9. **travels with my aunt**
   by graham greene
10. **rich man, poor man**
    by irwin shaw

Also...

Cartoonist Garry Trudeau's **Doonesbury** premiered in U.S. papers. Ursula Le Guin, **The Lathe of Heaven**. C. P. Snow, **Public Affairs**, a collection of essays. Saul Bellow, **Mr. Sammler's Planet**. Kurt Vonnegut wrote his play **Happy Birthday, Wanda June**. Agatha Christie killed off Hercule Poirot in **Curtain**. Kate Millett published **Sexual Politics**. Theodore Roszak published **The Making of a Counter-Culture**.

books

nonfiction

1. **everything you always wanted to know about sex**
   by david reuben, m.d.
2. **the new english bible**
3. **the sensuous woman**
   by "j" (pseudonym)
4. **better homes and gardens fondue and tabletop cooking**
5. **up the organization**
   by robert townsend
6. **ball four**
   by jim bouton
7. **american heritage dictionary of the english language**
8. **body language**
   by julius fast
9. **in someone's shadow**
   by rod mckuen (poetry, sort of)
10. **caught in the quiet**
    ditto, ditto.

ERNEST HEMINGWAY

The first New York Marathon was held September 13; Gary Muhrcke came in first with a time of 2 hours, 31 minutes, 38.2 seconds. Of the 126 starters, 55 finished the course.

final factoid

"Ecology" was the buzzword, and this gave new impetus to fake furs. Animal and reptile prints flourished, in underwear, swimwear, and evening dresses as well.

Pants were no longer controversial for women. They went everywhere, including to work.

The dog collar or choker was an important accessory — in velvet ribbon, Indian beads, or even rhinestones. The Ethnic Influence was a major trend. Native American, Gypsy, cowboy, Victorian, and other exotic styles were hugely popular.

Menswear continued to grow bolder. Wider lapels, more indented waistlines, longer vents in jackets; hero-sized stripes for shirtings. Striped shirts worn with striped suits. Ruffled shirts.

fashion

TIE-DYED EVERYTHING FOR EVERYONE

In kids' wear, the trend was to let children be children again. Bell-bottom jeans and sailor pants for boys. Pleats, dirndls, and ginghams for girls.

Some popular cars and their prices:

Datsun 1200 — $1,736
VW Beetle — $1,780
Toyota Corolla — $1,798
AMC Gremlin two-passenger sedan — $1,899
VW Super Beetle — $1,899
Ford Pinto — $1,919
Gremlin 4–passenger — $1,999
Chevy Vega 2–door — $2,091

American auto producers suffered a major setback in 1970. Only the lowest-priced compacts sold well. Consumers focused on lower prices and were often turning to imports. New American compacts were introduced to compete with the VW Beetle, Toyota Corolla, and other imports. The Chevy Vega and Ford Pinto, both 4-cylinder models, joined the AMC Gremlin. Dodge offered the Demon.

cars

Car producers adjusted their engines to use the new low-lead or lead-free gasolines. New models were forced to carry an emission-reducing system.

The Super Beetle.

VOLKSWAGEN OFFERED THE SUPER BEETLE, 3.2 INCHES LONGER THAN THE ORIGINAL.

Patton was the big winner, as Best Picture, for its script, for **Franklin Schaffner's** direction, and for **George C. Scott**, who was named Best Actor, but declined the award. Other nominees for Best Picture were *Airport, Five Easy Pieces, Love Story,* and *M*A*S*H.* Other Best Actor nominees were Melvyn Douglas for *I Never Sang for My Father*, James Earl Jones in *The Great White Hope* (a role he had originated on Broadway), Jack Nicholson for *Five Easy Pieces*, and Ryan O'Neal in *Love Story*. **Glenda Jackson** won Best Actress Oscar for *Women in Love*. **John Mills** received Supporting-Actor honors for *Ryan's Hope*, and **Helen Hayes** won for her role in *Airport*. Screenwriting awards went to **Coppola** for *Patton* and **Ring Lardner, Jr.**, for *M*A*S*H.* **Frank Sinatra** was awarded the Jean Hersholt Humanitarian Award. The Italian movie ***Investigation of a Citizen Above Suspicion*** was Best Foreign-Language Film. "For All We Know," from *Lovers and Other Strangers*, was Best Song. Best Original Song Score went to the Beatles for ***Let It Be***.

The top-earning film was
1. **Airport,** which grossed $37,650,796.
2. **M*A*S*H** earned $22 million
3. **Patton,** $21 million
4. **Bob & Carol & Ted & Alice**
5. **Woodstock**
6. **Hello, Dolly!**
7. **Cactus Flower**
8. **Catch–22**
9. **On Her Majesty's Secret Service**
10. **The Reivers**

THE AVERAGE COST OF A MOVIE TICKET WAS $1.55.

BOB & CAROL & TED & ALICE

movies

Tom Seaver of the New York Mets tied the major-league strikeout record of 19 in one game, 10 of them in a row. The record had been set in 1969 by Phillie Steve Carlton.

Jockey **Willie Shoemaker** set a new world record for winning mounts — he won his 6033rd race September 7.

Billie Jean King and **Rosemary Casals** triumphed at Wimbledon, in women's doubles, for the 3rd time in 4 years. Casals paired with Rumanian Ilie Nastase to win the mixed doubles. Margaret Smith Court of Australia beat Billie Jean in the women's finals in a match that lasted 2 1/2 hours.

Joe Frazier knocked out Jimmy Ellis on February 16, ending a three-year-old controversy over the world heavyweight title.

sports '70

Super Bowl IV was won by the Kansas City Chiefs, who defeated the Minnesota Vikings 23–7.

THE AMERICA'S CUP WAS SUCCESSFULLY DEFENDED BY THE U.S. YACHT *INTREPID.*

The Beatles broke up.

archive photos: inside frontcover, pages 1, 10, 22, 23, inside backcover

associated press: pages 2, 3, 4, 5, 6, 11, 15, 17, 24, 25

photofest: pages 8, 9, 13, 18, 19

marathon photo: ruth orkin
new york runner club

photo research:
alice albert

coordination:
rustyn birch

design:
carol bokuniewicz design
paul ritter